I AM...

A Bright Rainbow

A Story of Life Force Energy, Mindful Presence, and Magnificent YOU

LORAINE G. MÁDIAN

Balboa Press books may be ordered through booksellers or by contacting:

Balboa Press
A Division of Hay House
1663 Liberty Drive
Bloomington, IN 47403
www.balboapress.com
844-682-1282

Because of the dynamic nature of the Internet, any web addresses or links contained
in this book may have changed since publication and may no longer be valid. The views
expressed in this work are solely those of the author and do not necessarily reflect the views
of the publisher, and the publisher hereby disclaims any responsibility for them.

Any people depicted in stock imagery provided by Getty Images are models,
and such images are being used for illustrative purposes only.
Certain stock imagery © Getty Images.

Interior Image Credit: Illustrations by Gabrielle E. Rouhier

Photos by: Micaela Houston

ISBN: 979-8-7652-2511-0 (sc)
ISBN: 979-8-7652-2513-4 (hc)
ISBN: 979-8-7652-2512-7 (e)

Library of Congress Control Number: 2022909213

Print information available on the last page.

Balboa Press rev. date: 07/12/2022

BALBOA.PRESS
A DIVISION OF HAY HOUSE

ACKNOWLEDGEMENTS

This book is based on research and observation of the chakra system. I am thankful for a number of incredible friends, colleagues, and clients who were a significant part of the journey to publish this work. To those who wrote the praises, your contribution is appreciated. B. Hampton, thank you for your poetic writing suggestions. Gabrielle Rouhier, your illustrations are a beautiful compliment. Shahn McGuire and Michael Malone, your teachings, wisdom, and mentorship are invaluable. I would like to acknowledge gratitude for the love and support of my family: my beautiful mother Gisele and to my amazing, grown children, Skyler and Roxanna. Primarily, I am acknowledging God, known also as the Universe or the Divine, for blessing me as a channel to send a powerful message.

PRAISE FOR I AM ... A BRIGHT RAINBOW

"This is an incredibly well-crafted piece. It is very visual. It tells us that others experience the same as us-helps us connect. For younger readers this is very important, because they don't have the maturity to know that what they are feeling is very normal."

—MC, Washington State third grade educator

*"**B**efore I read I AM... A Bright Rainbow, I didn't have a grasp on chakras, but from an engineer perspective, it makes sense that "me" not the meat suit, is all electro magnetic signals (frequencies). Almost all of these frequencies are undetectable by our senses, but they are there as demonstrated by radios, internet and the like. The energy we are unaware of impacts us both plus and minus, but we are unaware and are tossed around like a boat in a storm, just at its mercy. **A**fter reading, the story breaks it down really well. It was very relaxing-the white light illuminating all of my colors. I felt like it was happening, a new and interesting sensation."*

—Thomas, age sixty-four

*"**B**efore reading I AM... A Bright Rainbow, I am feeling neutral with a little exhaustion. I think my third eye is open, but I don't know about the rest of my chakras. Life is pretty chaotic and stressful.*

After reading, I now know for a long time of my life, my throat chakra was closed and I was unable to speak up when I could or say my truth. I feel very open and grounded. I feel calm. I feel safe. I am more able to say the things I can and be able to talk to people more. I feel more educated on the chakras and energies. I feel relaxed and hopeful. The universe gives faith and hope."

—Molly, age fourteen

"Before reading I AM... A Bright Rainbow, I feel a little tired and nervous. After reading, I feel more at peace with myself and the world around me. I have a better understanding of how I can be true to myself. The content of the story is amazing. I liked how visual it was. I was very in the moment. Being in the moment helps me, because I am able to step back and understand nothing bad is happening NOW."

—Bella, age fourteen

"Before reading I AM... A Bright Rainbow, I feel sad, exhausted, my OCD is triggered and I feel uncomfy. Something needs to be fixed. After reading, I have acceptance. I am true to myself and embrace the world. The universe has a path for me and everything that is happening is happening for me not against me."

—Baleigh, age twenty

"Before reading I AM... A Bright Rainbow, I feel sad, very sad and I see black. After reading, I was happier. I think I see light at the end of the maze. Thanks for showing me color."

—Sophia, age eleven

INTRODUCTION

We observe young children as mostly present, joyful, expansive, and active with vital energy. They are in the flow, experiencing positive emotions in the moment, seeing the world with newness, magic, and creativity. They express this with their rainbow artwork.

Sophia, age eleven, writes, "Rainbows remind me of the world. When I see one, I believe happy things are under it and the blessings. It brings people together."

I AM... A Bright Rainbow will provide tools to help you interpret your body. Attuning to the chakra system will realign and direct your energy in a conscious way. With intentionality, we can all continue to shine our bright rainbow light.

For Alicea, a forever-bright rainbow,

and to magnificent YOU!

free

This is a story of my life.
My world is created in colors.
The energy surrounds me
and flows through me.

When I connect to my Self,
moment after moment,
here and now,
my world is magical and ... free.

And so it is.

I AM ... Safe

Red is the first color in my rainbow.

I am alive, like cherries in the trees.

I am rooted to the earth,
grounded, full, and open.

I remember this.

Red secures me.

I AM ... Creative

The orange energy is swirling.

I feel my many emotions,
though they are never the same shape.
They pass like clouds in the sky.

I am my dreams and my hopes.

I am in control of my Self.
I am the creator of a life I love.

Orange creates me.

Yellow fills my soul and nourishes me.

I trust in myself.

I can choose
what to be aware of,
zoom into, and focus on.

I am confident.
I am courageous!

Yellow strengthens me.

I AM ... Love

Green lives through me
and through everything.

I am guided by my heart.

I love and accept myself
and all parts of me.

Green blesses me.

I AM ... My Voice

Blue is the color of the sea and the sky.

I am safe to speak.
I let go and express myself.
I can say what I think and feel.
I ask for what I want and need.

Blue frees me.

I AM ... Connected

Purple is the color of gemstones.

My emotions are my compass that guides me.

I use my intuition, inspiration and imagination
to open doors to my purpose.

Purple awakens me.

I AM ... Energy

Pure,
like the pearls of the ocean,
neither always seen nor forgotten.

It is the never-ending flow.

I imagine a
bright-white light above my head
I tune in.

I AM ... part of all that is.

The rainbow life energy is flowing,
balanced, through my body.

I am connected to my inner Self
and to my outer surroundings.

Life is a fascination and my adventure!

But sometimes ...

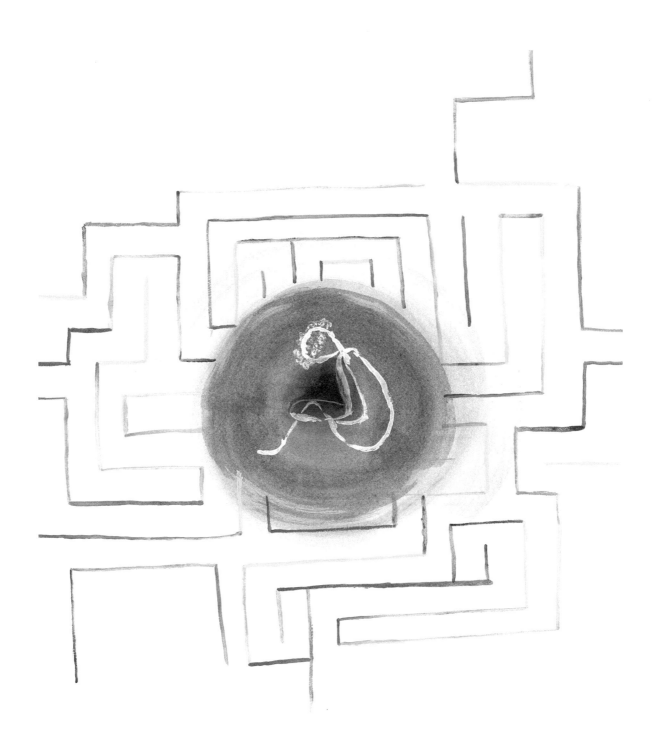

Life becomes too much!

The playground of Earth
can be messy and tough to navigate,
like a confusing maze.

I find myself becoming overwhelmed, frustrated,
angry, hateful, sad, or afraid.

I feel disconnected. What is in my way?
Have I become a shadow of myself—
closed, cold, tightly wound,
unforgiving, ungrateful?

The flow of life energy in my body just stops.
It is blocked, and the pressure is building;
it is heavy, and my colors are dimmed.
The dark energy encloses and imprisons me.

Trapped somewhere in the future,
I think about what could be next and worry.
Or trapped in the past,
I have memories of what happened before now.

I know this is not who I am fully.

And I remember to remind myself
that this means I am alive.

I close my eyes.
I breathe in and out all the way.

I let go of negative thoughts or expectations.
I use my will to rise above what I cannot control.

I realign with my Self
and step into the present.

I become still.
In this moment,
there is certainty,
and all is well.

And guess what happens.

Like a rainbow after a storm,
my colors brighten.

I open my energy channels,
and with this spaciousness and flow,
I surrender to my brilliance.

I have attuned to my chakra alignment.

I AM ... Safe

First, I focus on my root chakra.
It is located at the base of my spine, my tailbone.
This glowing red sphere is spinning.
It is vibrant, vital, and bold.

I breathe deeply now.
With each breath, there is a clearing.

I have conscious awareness.

I am more rooted to the earth,
part of an intricate web,
connected to the core that supports
all that lives.

I absorb life energy
and become nourished.

I learn and I grow
by withstanding challenges.

I imagine red.
I feel relief and belonging,
secure and solid
in my being in this moment.

I AM ... Creative

I tune into my navel chakra.
I visualize an orange vortex of spiraling energy.

I inhale life energy directly into my chakra.
And I allow the energy to expand.

I breathe more fully and with ease now.

I release my worries.
I let go of self-doubt,
disappointment,
shame, and blame.

I befriend curiosity.
I can sense possibility and newness.

I am open and flexible.

I imagine orange.
I feel inspiration and joy.

When opened, my yellow chakra is brilliant,
like the sun rising and setting.

I breathe energy into my center chakra.
And I allow it to brighten and widen
with each breath.

What thoughts, words, actions,
and experiences can meet my needs?

I have many opportunities.
I know my limits and boundaries.
How and with whom
do I want to exchange energy?

I intentionally follow my inner knowing,
and my behaviors match for my highest good.

I am confident in my self-worth.

I imagine yellow.
I feel my personal power.

I AM ... Loving Kindness

I place my hand on my heart center.
I see beautiful green.

Warmth moves through every cell of my body.

I drop my walls.
I let the loneliness float away.

I experience forgiveness.

I discover the lessons and create meaning as a
portal to healing and compassion.

My heart is opening like a blooming flower.

I give love and receive love
from an authentic place.

I imagine green.
I feel gratitude, generosity, and benevolence.

I AM ... Expressive

I see the color blue.

When lies and secrets close my throat chakra,
I can be choked up, shut down, and go silent.
Or I want to scream and yell!

I swallow and clear my throat.

I can stand up for myself,
giving voice to my inner wisdom.

Like the sounds of the ocean,
I know my words need to be heard.

I imagine blue.
I think positive thoughts.
I feel free.

I AM ... Connected

Purple is in the center of my forehead.

If I feel confused by illusions,
judgments, and projections,
I can focus on my third-eye chakra.

I breathe directly into my chakra.
And I allow for the expansion.

The foggy veil is lifted.

I see my own truth.
I am open to consider others' perceptions
with discernment.

I have awoken.
I have complete awareness now.

I am in the right place at the right timing.

I imagine purple.
I sense my intuition and have clarity.

I AM ... Energy

Open to the Divine source,
I align with the white light
above my head.

The glowing light is flowing through me, like a
waterfall, illuminating all my colors.
And with the passing wave,
I am renewed and made whole.

As I connect to the current
that runs through all life,
this universal light channel is
my force, my liberation,
and all that lives within me.

Now I can be patient and trusting
in the unfolding of events.
And so I have curiosity and courage
to journey on my path out to the unknown
with faith and hope.

I embrace the great mystery
and am in wonder of miracles;
I am part of this abundant universe,
supported by unseen forces.

I feel inner calmness, harmony, and bliss.

My own rainbow speaks to the universe
with its exquisite colorful light.

The universe shines back at me.
And I receive the reflection of
my own radiant bright light.

And so it is.

I AM … a masterpiece,
the artist of my magnificent rainbow.

The health of our chakras is directly related to the health of our physical body, our mind and our emotions. **I AM... A Bright Rainbow** helps us to learn to keep these energy centers (vital life force) open and unblocked, keeping us vibrant, healthy, and feeling alive.

We can refer to color as a universal language; for example, a rainbow provides calmness and beauty after a storm. It is stated that the colorful chakra system originated in India in the Vedas, the oldest text (between 1500 and 500 BC). The word *chakra* in Sanskrit translates to a wheel or disk of energy. The seven chakras are located from the top of the head (referred to as the *crown)* to the base of the spine (the *root*). The lower chakras are related to earthly concerns of survival and power. The upper chakras are associated with higher consciousness of truth, intuition, and purpose. The middle heart chakra translating to love and compassion can be considered a bridge joining the two worlds. Chakra healing is an intentional practice of connecting with stored energy.

Each sphere is a spinning vortex of invisible healing energy running along the spine and expanding through and past all sides of the physical body. Each energy center is an organizing structure that receives, assimilates, and expresses life energy, vibrating at a certain frequency and responding to different wavelengths of light. Each disk of spiraling, flowing energy connects to a certain color, nerve bundle, and major organ. As emotions of the body change, the chakra colors also change. If a chakra becomes blocked and movement stops, energy cannot flow. Each chakra can be seen, felt, and sensed with intuition. We can observe the open or closed status of a chakra with a pendulum placed over the chakra to demonstrate movement of energy flow.

Albert Einstein (early 1900s) announced his discovery that energy is neither created or destroyed. He said that *energy in the universe is constant and can only be changed from one form to another.* "Everything is energy, and that's all there is to it. Match the frequency of the reality you want, and you cannot help but get that reality. It can be no other way. This is not philosophy. This is physics."

In summary, the chakras are a *superpower,* a gateway to the intimate connection between cosmic energy / God and Self (the soul, the mind, emotions and the body). When we can shift our energy by aligning with and opening our chakras, we can attune to a unified field. In surrendering to this, we are infinite, unbounded, and balanced, and this affects our whole well-being.

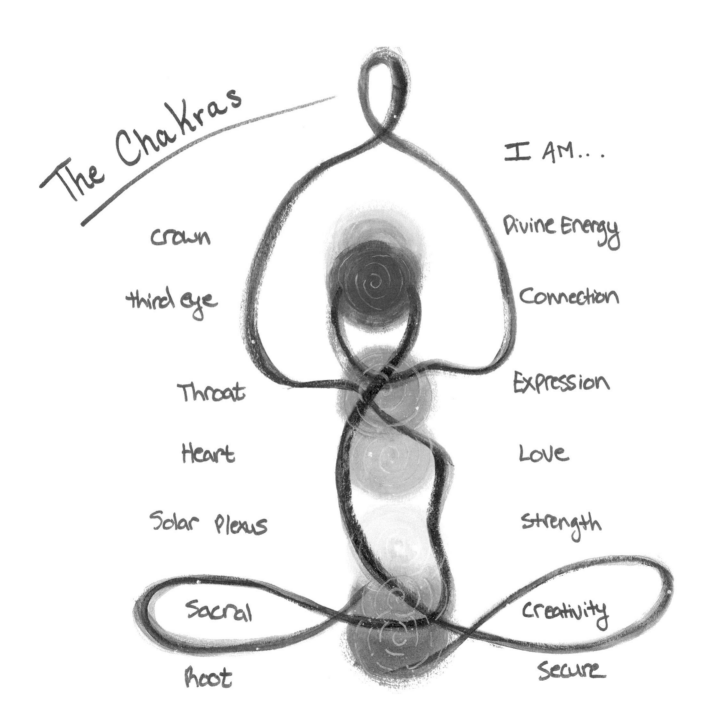

The ChaKras

I AM...

crown   Divine Energy

third eye   Connection

Throat   Expression

Heart   Love

Solar Plexus   Strength

Sacral   Creativity

Root   Secure

Printed in the United States
by Baker & Taylor Publisher Services